Lamb of God

Pauline Shone

Published by Zaccmedia
www.zaccmedia.com
info@zaccmedia.com

Published December 2013

ISBN: 978-1-909824-04-1

British Library Cataloguing-in-Publication Data
A catalogue record for this book is available from the British Library

CONTENTS

**This book is dedicated to the memory of
Lydia and Derek Prince**

Lydia's true-life story, 'Appointment in Jerusalem', written by her husband Derek Prince, was instrumental in leading me to a personal faith in the Jewish Messiah.

Lydia's personal experiences and Derek's prophetic insights from Scripture were valuable foundations on which to build an understanding of Israel. Events that take place in this tiny country are of worldwide significance.

FOREWORD

Pauline Shone has done a very good and creative job in collecting and briefly commentating on the key Messianic Biblical prophecies. I am sure this book, helpfully divided into fourteen chapters, will be a highly valued introductory resource in many evangelistic, teaching and devotional contexts.

It is always encouraging to our understanding and our faith to see the unfolding of God's purposes throughout history, so clearly stated in Scripture. As the truths of Scripture are presented our thankfulness for the faithfulness of God in the past and present increases, also our hope and trust for the future is renewed.

Rev Alex Jacob M.A, M.PHIL –
CEO, The Churches Ministry
Among Jews

INTRODUCTION

The first ten chapters of this book follow a thread of key messianic Biblical prophecies that foretell the coming of the Messiah. It also studies the events that exactly fulfilled these promises, recorded in the Bible and verified by reliable witnesses.

The last two chapters cover some of the future Biblical prophecies relating to Messiah's return, and their possible course of fulfillment.

Only God Himself knows the exact times and seasons of all the Biblical prophecies and complex events yet to take place. However, as they will all be fulfilled in Israel, it is very significant that the Jewish people are back in the land of their forefathers.

CHAPTER ONE

THE FIRST PROPHECY CONCERNING MESSIAH

SEED OF A WOMAN

> *"And I will put enmity*
> *Between you and the woman,*
> *And between your seed and **her Seed**;*
> *He shall bruise your head,*
> *And you shall bruise His heel."*
>
> (GENESIS 3:15, EMPHASIS ADDED)

God had told Adam and Eve that they could eat the fruit from every tree in the Garden of Eden, with one exception. He warned them not to eat from the tree of the knowledge of good and evil that was in the middle of the garden; if they ate its fruit they would die.

The serpent came to Eve and introduced doubt about what God had actually stated. Then he contradicted God's word, saying that they would not die if they ate the forbidden fruit. He also questioned God's motives for the restriction; saying that He knew their eyes would be opened when they ate and they would become like God, knowing good and evil.

The temptation to disobey God and ignore His warning was initiated by Satan, and listening to Satan's skillful lies led to rebellion against God's commandment. Because of what he had done, the serpent was cursed by God. He also declared that there would be enmity between Satan and the woman; and between Satan's seed and the woman's Seed.

Her Seed would eventually defeat Satan's seed, but Satan would cause Him great suffering. As Biblical society was strictly patriarchal and generations were traced through fathers and sons, the phrase 'her Seed' is unique.

CHAPTER TWO

PROPHECIES CONCERNING MESSIAH'S EARTHLY ANCESTRY

SEED OF ABRAHAM, ISAAC AND JACOB

"Blessed be the LORD,
The God of Shem,
And may Canaan be his servant.
May God enlarge Japheth,
And may he dwell in the tents of Shem;
And may Canaan be his servant."

(GENESIS 9:26-27)

After the flood, when the earth was dried, God told Noah and his family to leave the ark. He also instructed him to bring out all the living creatures. Then Noah built an altar to the LORD and made a burnt offering on it. The sacrifice was pleasing and acceptable to God. He promised that He would

3

not curse the earth again and destroy all living things with a flood.

He blessed Noah and his sons Shem, Ham, the father of Canaan, and Japheth; the fathers of three new nations after the Flood, populating the earth.

Noah planted a vineyard and after becoming drunk on the wine, he lay uncovered in his tent. Ham looked at his father's nakedness; but Shem and Japheth walked backwards with a covering for their father, turning their faces to avoid seeing him. Afterwards Noah blessed his sons Shem and Japheth. As Ham had already been blessed by God, Noah cursed him indirectly by cursing his son Canaan.

Shem is given precedence over Noah's other sons and it was God's choice that Messiah would come from the line of Shem, the Semitic race.

"I will make you a great nation;
I will bless you
And make your name great;
And you shall be a blessing.
I will bless those who bless you,
And I will curse him who curses you;
And in you all the families of the earth shall be blessed."

(GENESIS 12:2-3)

God commanded Abram, a descendant of Shem, to leave his country, his family and his tribe, for a land that He would show him. God blessed Abram and promised that he would become the father of a great nation.

Abram obeyed God and eventually became the father of the Jewish nation. God changed Abram's name to Abraham, meaning father of many nations. He is also the father of Ishmael and the Arab peoples, as well as people groups descended from children borne to him by Keturah.

It was God's foreordained plan that Messiah's nationality would be Jewish and that He would be a blessing to all the nations on earth.

But God said to Abraham, "Do not let it be displeasing in your sight because of the lad or because of your bondwoman. Whatever Sarah has said to you, listen to her voice; for in Isaac your seed shall be called."

(GENESIS 21:12)

When Abraham and his wife Sarah were old, God promised them a son. Sarah miraculously conceived when she was well past the age of childbearing and Isaac was born.

Now Abraham had a firstborn son named Ishmael, who had been borne to him by his wife's Egyptian handmaid Hagar. But there was enmity between Sarah and her son, and Ishmael and Hagar. So Sarah insisted that Abraham send them away.

Of course Abraham loved Ishmael and was troubled about this. Then God spoke to him directly, instructing him to listen to his wife. He would bless Ishmael and make him into a great nation. But it was His sovereign choice that the messianic line would continue through Isaac, the son of the promise.

"I see Him, but not now;
I behold Him, but not near;
A Star shall come out of Jacob;
A Scepter shall rise out of Israel,

> *And batter the brow of Moab,*
> *And destroy all the sons of tumult."*

(NUMBERS 24:17)

Isaac's wife Rebekah was pregnant and her babies struggled together in the womb. So Rebekah asked the LORD what was happening. He told her that there were two nations in her womb. One people would be stronger than the other and the older would serve the younger.

Esau was the first twin to be born and then Jacob, who grasped his brother's heel. Esau grew and became a skillful hunter in the fields. But Jacob was a quiet man, dwelling in tents. Esau despised his firstborn rights and sold them to Jacob for a bowl of stew. He also married Hittite women who believed in many gods, causing his parents great distress.

When Isaac was dying, Rebekah encouraged Jacob to trick his father into giving him the firstborn's blessing. This caused enmity between the brothers. Fearing for Jacob's life, Rebekah sent him to her brother Laban in Haran. Yet it was God's will that His promises to Abraham and Isaac would be inherited by Jacob, not his firstborn son Esau.

Jacob married Leah and Rachel, the daughters of Laban. Children were also borne to him by Rachel's maidservant Bilhah and Leah's maidservant Zilpah. Jacob's life was very difficult, but God's blessing was continually upon him. He changed Jacob's name to Israel, meaning 'Prince with God.'

> *"The scepter[1] shall not depart from Judah,*
> *Nor a lawgiver from between his feet,*

---

[1] Scepter – a symbol of kingship

> *Until Shiloh (*Messiah) comes;*
> *And to Him shall be the obedience of the people."*
>
> (GENESIS 49:10, *AUTHOR'S NOTE)

In his last days Jacob gathered his twelve sons around him and spoke to them individually. Beginning with his firstborn Reuben, he declared what would happen to them in the future. Jacob praised Judah greatly, saying that he was like a mighty lion and would rise to leadership over the twelve sons. In blessing Judah, he predicts that a royal line would rise from his descendants and rule until Shiloh (Messiah) came.

Jacob also blessed and praised Joseph, the son who had been betrayed by his brothers. Joseph had developed great strength of character and the Mighty God of Jacob had been his protection. He described Joseph as being separated to serve God's holy purposes.

God had selected Jacob's son Judah, whose name means 'Praise'. It was God's choice that the Messiah-King would come from the tribe of Judah.

SON OF DAVID

> *Of the increase of His government and peace*
> *There will be no end,*
> *Upon the throne of David and over His kingdom,*
> *To order it and establish it with judgment and justice*
> *From that time forward, even forever.*
> *The zeal of the LORD of hosts will perform this.*
>
> (ISAIAH 9:7)

7

There shall come forth a Rod from the stem of Jesse,
And a Branch shall grow out of his roots.

(ISAIAH 11:1)

Led by Joshua, the children of Israel invaded Canaan, conquered the people and took possession of the land. Each tribe of Israel received a portion of the land as their inheritance.

Under the godly leadership of Joshua, the Israelites were faithful to the God of Israel. After Joshua's death Israel was led by judges and during this period the Israelites turned from God's law. Everyone did what they considered to be right by their own standards. For nearly four centuries there were repeated cycles of rebellion against God, leading to defeat by their enemies and then a return to God.

Samuel was the last judge and the first prophet. During his godly leadership there was a transition from judges to kings. The Israelites no longer wanted God to reign over them; they wanted to be like the other nations and have a king to rule over them.

Saul was anointed by Samuel to be the first king of Israel. But, although His outward appearance was impressive, he was not fully obedient to God's commandments. Eventually God regretted that He had made Saul king.

God told Samuel to take anointing oil and go to Jesse the Bethlehemite; because He had chosen a king from one of his sons. From the many tribes of Judah, God chose David, the youngest son of Jesse; to be the anointed king of Israel and an ancestor of Messiah, the Eternal King.

Saul had lost God's blessing and was jealous of David's anointing. There was enmity between them throughout the remainder of Saul's reign. The king continually persecuted

David, until his death in battle with the Philistines. The future king had to live as a fugitive, fighting for his survival. Yet David would not harm Saul, even when he was given the opportunity to do so.

David was a courageous warrior and he gathered many followers during his years of exile. The LORD sees what is inside the heart of man and He knew that David loved Him wholeheartedly.

After Saul's death, David was anointed by the men of Judah as their king. He reigned over them in Hebron for seven and a half years. Then he was anointed as king over all the tribes of Israel. From Jerusalem, David reigned over all Israel and Judah for thirty-three years.

FULFILMENT AND EVIDENCE

Jews kept meticulous records and all public registers were carefully preserved. Two genealogies are recorded in the Bible concerning Jesus' birth.

Matthew's Gospel records Jesus' genealogy from Abraham, Isaac, and Jacob; and traces His legal inheritance line through David's son Solomon.

Luke's Gospel records Jesus' genealogy from Joseph, all the way back to Adam, and His royal blood line through Nathan, another son of David.

It could be that Matthew traced Joseph's line and Luke traced Mary's line. Joseph and Mary were most probably of the same tribe and family, according to the Jewish Law (Numbers 36:8).

CHAPTER THREE

PROPHECIES CONCERNING A FORERUNNER

The voice of one crying in the wilderness:
"Prepare the way of the LORD;
Make straight in the desert
A highway for our God."

(ISAIAH 40:3)

"Behold, I send My messenger,
And he will prepare the way before Me.
And the Lord, whom you seek,
Will suddenly come to His temple,
Even the Messenger of the covenant,
In whom you delight.
Behold, He is coming,"
Says the LORD of hosts.

(MALACHI 3:1)

Prophecies concerning a forerunner, who would precede the coming of Messiah and prepare His way, were well known among Jews. After the time of the prophet Malachi no other prophets had appeared in Israel and there was a period of silence lasting about 400 years. Then John the Baptist came as God's messenger, to prepare the people of Israel for the promised Messiah.

FULFILMENT

From 37 B.C. to 4 B.C. Judea, Samaria and Galilee were governed by Rome. Herod the Great, half-Idumaean and half-Israelite, was appointed under Roman patronage and ruled as king over Judea.

The Jews deeply resented the Roman occupation and hated the ruthlessly ambitious King Herod. Their only hope for liberation was centred on God's prophecies of a Messiah; a King who would reign over Israel forever on the throne of David.

During the time that King Herod was ruling in Judea, there was a certain priest named Zechariah, of the division of Abijah. He and his wife were righteous Jews, who loved God and kept the requirements of the Law. They had no children, as Elizabeth was barren and they were both old. One day, when Zechariah's division was serving at the temple in Jerusalem, he was chosen by lot to burn incense to the LORD. This was a great honour, something that a priest could only do once in his career.

At the hour that the incense was offered and the people were praying outside the Temple, Zechariah was startled by the sudden appearance of an angel, standing at the right side of the altar of incense.

The angel told him not to be afraid, his prayer had been heard. His wife Elizabeth would have a son and they were to name him John. He would be a prophet, consecrated to God and full of the Holy Spirit. He would go before Messiah in the spirit and power of Elijah; to turn the people back to God and prepare them for His coming.

But Zechariah, temporarily forgetting God's supernatural ability to fulfill His promises, looked at his natural circumstances and struggled to believe this incredible announcement.

The angel said that his name was Gabriel and that he had been sent by God. Because Zechariah had doubted his message, he would be mute until the promise was fulfilled.

WITNESSES

The people waiting outside wondered why Zechariah was taking so long in the temple. When he came out he could not speak to them and they perceived he had seen a vision.

FULFILMENT

After Zechariah had completed his days of service at the temple, he returned home. Later his wife Elizabeth conceived and she withdrew for the first five months of her pregnancy. When it was time for her to give birth, she had a boy and on the eight day they came to circumcise him. Everyone expected the baby to be named Zechariah, but Elizabeth said that his name was John.

Her relatives and neighbours were surprised; as it was the custom to name a child after a relative and no one in the family had that name. As Zechariah was deaf and mute they made signs to him, to find out what he would like the baby to be named.

Zechariah asked for a writing tablet and wrote, "His name is John." Immediately Zechariah was able to talk again and began praising God. Everyone living in the Judea area was filled with awe at these events and wondered what this child would be; because the hand of the LORD was with him.

Zechariah was filled with the Holy Spirit and prophesied, declaring that God's promise to send a Saviour from the family of David was now being fulfilled. John would be called the prophet of the Highest, because he would go before the LORD to prepare His way; giving knowledge of salvation to His people by the remission of their sins.

The child grew and became strong in spirit. He lived in the desert until he came out to preach to Israel.

Chapter Four

Prophecies Concerning Messiah's Birth

Immanuel

"Therefore the Lord Himself shall give you a sign: Behold, the virgin shall conceive and bear a Son, and shall call His name Immanuel."

(Isaiah 7:14)

God had promised a sign to the house of David. A virgin would give birth to a Son, whose name would be Immanuel, 'God-With-Us.'

This prophecy speaks of a man born of a woman, but independently of man, a biological impossibility. But as God created the universe out of nothing and man from the dust of the ground, He could certainly bring about a virgin birth.

Fulfilment

Six months after Elizabeth's conception God sent the angel Gabriel to a city of Galilee named Nazareth, to a virgin named Mary. Entering her home, Gabriel greeted Mary, telling her to rejoice! She was highly favoured, the Lord was with her and she was blessed among women.

Mary was shaken by the angel's visitation and confused by his greeting; but the angelic visitor reassured Mary, saying that he had come with a message from God.

Mary would conceive and give birth to a Son. His name would be JESUS. He would be great and called the **Son of God**. The Lord God would give Him the throne of His ancestor David and He would rule over Jacob's house forever. Mary believed the message, but struggled to comprehend how it could be accomplished. Gabriel explained that the Holy Spirit would come upon her and she would conceive by the power of God.

Then Gabriel told Mary that her relative Elizabeth had conceived a son and she was now six months pregnant; even though she was old and everyone had thought she was barren. Mary knew that her reputation would be at stake, but asking no questions, she humbly surrendered to the plan and purpose of God.

Witnesses: Elizabeth and John

Soon afterwards, Mary visited Elizabeth her cousin. At the sound of her greeting, the baby jumped for joy in Elizabeth's womb and she was filled with the Holy Spirit. Before Mary could share her news, Elizabeth already knew that she had been chosen to be the mother of the LORD. She declared that Mary was blessed among women and the fruit of her womb was blessed. She marveled at the privilege of Mary's visit and said those things promised to her would come to pass; because she had believed.

Chapter Five

Prophecies Concerning Messiah's Birthplace

Bethlehem

"But you, **Bethlehem Ephrathah,**
Though *you are little among the thousands of Judah,*
Yet out of you shall come forth to Me
The One to be Ruler in Israel,
Whose goings forth are from of old,
From everlasting."

(Micah 5:2, emphasis added)

Fulfilment

Now Mary was engaged to Joseph, a direct descendant of King David. When he discovered Mary was pregnant, it appeared that she had betrayed him. Bitterly disappointed, he wanted to break off the engagement. But being a good man and a devout Jew, he desired to do it discreetly; so that Mary would not be shamed and disgraced.

While Joseph was grappling with this dilemma, God's angel spoke to him in a dream, telling him to marry Mary, as the Baby had been conceived by the Holy Spirit of God. She would have a Son and He was to be named JESUS, meaning Saviour; because He would save the people from their sins.

Overawed by the mystery of Mary having been chosen to be the mother of the Saviour King, Joseph's concerns were banished.

He did as the angel had commanded and married Mary as originally planned; but the marriage was not consummated until after the birth of her firstborn son. Joseph, of the lineage of David, was not the physical father of Jesus, but he became His legal father.

Mary and Joseph were living in Nazareth prior to the birth of Jesus. About that time, Caesar Augustus had ordered a census to be taken throughout the Roman Empire. In Israel it was customary to register at a person's ancestral home; so Joseph and Mary travelled to Bethlehem, the city of David.

While they were there, the time came for Jesus to be born. However, as Bethlehem was crowded with visitors registering for the census, there were no rooms left at the inn. So Jesus was born in a humble stable, wrapped in strips of cloth and laid in a manger.

WITNESSES: ANGELS

That night, there were shepherds in the fields nearby guarding their sheep. Suddenly an angel of God appeared to them and the light of God's glory shone around.

The angel told them not to be afraid, because he had some wonderful news for all people. That day a Saviour had been born in David's town, the Messiah and Ruler. He told the shepherds that they would find the Baby wrapped in pieces of cloth and lying in a manger.

Then a huge angelic choir joined the first angel, singing God's praises and giving Him glory, announcing peace toward all men and women on earth.

WITNESSES: SHEPHERDS

The shepherds quickly ran to Bethlehem. They found Joseph and Mary, and the Baby lying in a manger, just as the angel had said. After the shepherds had seen Him they spread the news of what had happened and everyone who heard their story was amazed.

WITNESS: SIMEON

On the eight day, to fulfill the Jewish Law, the Baby was circumcised and named JESUS. After Mary's days of purification were completed, they went to Jerusalem, to present their firstborn to God (Exodus 13:1-2).

Living in Jerusalem at that time was an old man named Simeon. He was a devout Jew, waiting expectantly for the coming of Israel's Messiah. It had been revealed to him by the Holy Spirit, that he would see the Messiah before he died. He was led by the Spirit to the Temple, just as Joseph and Mary arrived with Jesus, to carry out the rituals of the Jewish Law.

Simeon took Jesus up in his arms. He blessed God and said that the LORD would now let him depart in peace, for he had seen His salvation, a light of revelation to the Gentiles, and the glory of God's people Israel.

Jesus' father and mother marveled at the things that Simeon had spoken. Simeon blessed them, and he told Mary that there would be controversy in Israel concerning her Son and it would cause her pain, like a sword piercing her heart.

WITNESS: ANNA THE PROPHETESS

Anna was a widow and very old; she continually served God in the Temple with fasting and prayers. Seeing Simeon holding Jesus and praying, she also gave thanks to God for Him. Then she spoke about the Child to all who were waiting for national deliverance.

WITNESSES: THREE LEARNED MEN

Sometime after Jesus was born, learned men came from the East to Jerusalem. They had seen a supernatural star announcing the birth of the King of the Jews and had come to worship Him.

When King Herod heard of this he was deeply troubled. He gathered the Jewish religious scholars together and asked them where Messiah would be born. They answered that it was plainly written, by the prophet Micah, that Messiah would be born in Bethlehem.

Then Herod held a secret meeting with the wise men, to find out when the star had appeared. Afterwards he sent them to Bethlehem and told them to let him know when they found the Child, pretending that he also wanted to go and worship Him. The star they had followed from the east led them again and hovered over the exact place where the Child was. When they entered the house and saw the Child with His mother, they fell down and worshipped Him. Then they presented Him with gifts of gold, frankincense and myrrh.

The wise men were warned in a dream not to report back to Herod and they returned to their own country by another route.

An angel warned Joseph in a dream to take the Child and His mother to Egypt, because Herod would hunt for the Child and kill Him. Joseph left while it was dark, taking Mary and Jesus with him. The family remained in Egypt until after Herod's death.

CHAPTER SIX

PROPHECIES OF
MESSIAH'S PRE-EXISTENCE

EVERLASTING FATHER, PRINCE OF PEACE

"But you, Bethlehem Ephrathah,
Though *you are little among the thousands of Judah,*
Yet *out of you shall come forth to Me*
The One to be Ruler in Israel,
Whose goings forth* are *from of old,
From everlasting."

(MICAH 5:2, EMPHASIS ADDED)

"For unto us a Child is born,
Unto us a Son is given;
And the government will be upon His shoulder.
And His name will be called

22

Wonderful, Counselor, Mighty God,
Everlasting Father*, Prince of Peace.*"

(ISAIAH 9:6, EMPHASIS ADDED)

The promised Child was both human and divine. He would reign forever on the throne of David, something that God Himself promised to accomplish.

The LORD said to my Lord,
"Sit at My right hand,
Till I make Your enemies Your footstool."

(PSALM 110:1)

In writing this psalm David speaks of 'my Lord', someone greater than himself. Jesus was a descendant of David, yet his pre-existent LORD.

The apostle John omits any reference to the human descent of Jesus and begins his Gospel account with a bold and clear declaration of the deity of Jesus (John 1:1).

The divine and eternal Messiah existed before the earth and man were created. The LORD God's Anointed preceded all written prophecies and any recorded genealogies.

CHAPTER SEVEN

PROPHECY CONCERNING
A SACRIFICIAL LAMB

THE LAMB OF GOD

*And Abraham said, "My son, **God will provide for Himself the lamb for a burnt offering**."*

(GENESIS 22:8, EMPHASIS ADDED)

Adam and Eve sinned against God when they rebelled against His commandment. *And the LORD God commanded the man, saying, "Of every tree of the garden you may freely eat; but of the tree of the knowledge of good and evil you shall not eat, for **in the day that you eat of it you shall surely die**."* (Genesis 2:16-17, emphasis added). Sin and death entered humanity through their disobedience and man's nature became evil. Adam and Eve were ashamed of their nakedness and hid from God's presence. The serpent, Satan's tool, was cursed by God for instigating their sin. God also made a promise to Satan, that a Deliverer would come and destroy his evil works.

God did not excuse Eve's sin because she was deceived. He said that she would conceive and bear children in pain. And her husband would rule over her.

God cursed the ground because of Adam's sin. Thorns and thistles sprang up in the earth and Adam would experience heavy labour in providing food from the fields. Then he would eventually die and return to the dust of the earth from which he was made.

Yet God also showed Adam and Eve mercy. They had tried to cover their nakedness, but their self-efforts were inadequate. Before banishing them from the Garden of Eden, God made them clothing from animal skins; the first shedding of blood to provide covering.

The two sons of Eve brought offerings to God. Cain was a farmer and brought some of the produce of his toil. Abel was a shepherd and in faith he offered a sacrificed lamb, the first-born of his flock. Abel's offering was accepted by God. But God did not respect Cain and his offering. So Cain was very angry and, turning in enmity against Abel, he lured his brother into a field and murdered him.

Abel's sacrifice of a lamb made him righteous before God. It also speaks of Messiah, the Lamb of God. He would be sacrificed to make sinners righteous before God, enabling them to have an intimate relationship with Him and restoring what was lost by sin in the Garden of Eden.

God commanded Abraham to take his son Isaac and go to the land of Moriah, and offer Isaac there as a burnt offering on one of the mountains that God would show him. So Abraham obeyed and went to the place God had told him about, a three day journey.

Abraham told his servants to stay with the donkeys, while he and Isaac went to worship God. Then Abraham made a remarkable statement of faith, he said that they would return. As God had promised to create a nation through Isaac, Abraham reasoned that if he had to kill his son, God would bring him back to life.

The young man Isaac carried the wood for the burnt offering; Abraham carried the fire and the knife. As they went off together, Isaac asked his father where the lamb was for the sacrifice. And Abraham said that God Himself would provide the lamb for a burnt offering.

At the place God had appointed, Abraham built an altar and placed the wood on top. Then he tied Isaac and laid him on the wood. Just as Abraham was reaching for his knife, the Angel of the LORD called his name and commanded him to stop.

Then Abraham saw a ram caught in a bush by its horns and he sacrificed it as a burnt offering, instead of Isaac. Abraham had passed an extreme test of faith in not withholding his son, proving that he trusted God completely and would fully obey His commandments. Therefore God promised to bless him and give him many descendants.

In this literal event there was also a picture of a future event. The Messiah, Lamb of God, would be a burnt offering for the sins of all mankind.

"Now the blood shall be a sign for you on the houses where you are. And when I see the blood, I will pass over you; and the plague shall not be on you to destroy you when I strike the land of Egypt."

(EXODUS 12:13)

Pharaoh had obstinately refused every command of God to release the Israelites from their slavery in Egypt. As he continued to resist God, the series of warning plagues on Egypt became increasingly severe.

God sent Moses with a final warning. Every firstborn of the people and animals in the land of Egypt would die, but all the children of Israel would be saved from this disaster. Yet even then, Pharaoh would not relent.

God gave Moses instructions that would separate and preserve the children of Israel from God's judgment. Every man should take a healthy male lamb for his family. At twilight, on the fourteenth day of the first month, they were to kill the lamb and daub some of its blood on the door posts of their houses. The meat was to be roasted and eaten with unleavened bread and bitter herbs. They were to eat it in a hurry, dressed ready to leave.

God would pass through the land of Egypt that night and kill all the firstborn animals and people. He would also bring judgment on all the gods of Egypt. But when He saw the blood of the lamb on the houses He would pass over and the plague would not destroy them.

God ordained that the Passover feast was to be celebrated annually; and the story of God's protection and deliverance was to be faithfully related to each new generation.

After the LORD went through the land and killed the firstborn, Pharaoh released the children of Israel. Moses led them out of his kingdom, to serve the LORD God of Israel. Afterwards Pharaoh regretted that he had released his former slaves and pursued them to the Red Sea. But God miraculously parted the waters and made a way through the sea for His people to cross over. When they were safely on the other side, He brought the waters back together, drowning their enemies.

This actual event, when the blood of a lamb on the wooden door posts of the Israelites houses saved them from death, was also a picture of a future event. The atoning blood of the Messiah, shed on the wooden cross of His crucifixion, would separate and preserve from judgment all those who believed in Him, securing their eternal salvation.

Fulfilment

When Zechariah's son John finally burst onto the scene, prepared for his unique role and filled with the Holy Spirit, there was an excited and fervent messianic expectancy among the people. Eager crowds flocked to hear his fearless and fiery message of repentance, and many were baptized by him.

The Jewish leaders sent priests and Levites from Jerusalem to ask John who he was; and he told them that he was not the Messiah, or Elijah, or the Prophet. Under further pressure to identify who he was, John the Baptist claimed that he was the fulfilment of Isaiah's prophecy. He said, I am:

The voice of one crying in the wilderness:
"Prepare the way of the LORD;
Make straight in the desert
A highway for our God."

(ISAIAH 40:3)

Then the Pharisees questioned his authority to baptize. John answered that he baptized with water; but there was One standing among them who came after him, yet was higher in rank and he was not worthy to untie His sandals. John was witnessing to the pre-existence of Jesus. He was six months older than his cousin, yet he stated that Jesus was before him.

Witness: John the Baptist

The next day John saw Jesus coming toward him, and said, **"Behold! The Lamb of God who takes away the sin of the world!"**

(John 1:29, emphasis added)

Immediately after Jesus' baptism He was led by the Spirit into the wilderness, to be tempted by the devil. He fasted for forty days and nights and afterwards He was hungry. The tempter came to Him, saying, that if He was the Son of God, He should turn the stones into bread. But Jesus said: *"It is written, 'Man shall not live by bread alone, but by every word that proceeds from the mouth of God.'"* (Matthew 4:4, Deuteronomy 8:3)

Then the devil took Him to Jerusalem and put Him on top of the temple there, and said, *"If You are the Son of God, throw Yourself down. For it is written: 'He shall give His angels charge over you,' and, 'In their hands they shall bear you up, lest You dash your foot against a stone.'"* (Matthew 4:5, Psalm 91:11, 12)

Jesus answered, *"It is written again, 'You shall not tempt the Lord your God.'"* (Matthew 4:7, Deuteronomy 6:16)

Then the devil took Him to the peak of a very high mountain, and showed Him all the kingdoms of the world. He said that he would give them all to Jesus, if He would fall down and worship him.

Jesus said, *"Away with you, Satan! For it is written, 'You*

shall worship the LORD your God, and Him only you shall serve.'"
(Matthew 4:10, Deuteronomy 6:13)

Then Satan left Jesus, and angels came and took care of Him.

Adam had failed when tested, but Jesus triumphed over every temptation. Just as the lamb for the Passover feast had to be spotless, Jesus remained undefiled by sin. He resisted and defeated Satan with the Word of God.

CHAPTER EIGHT

PROPHECIES OF MESSIAH'S EARTHLY MINISTRY

By the way of the sea, beyond the Jordan,
In Galilee of the Gentiles.
The people who walked in darkness
Have seen a great light;
Those who dwelt in the land of the shadow of death,
Upon them a light has shined.

(ISAIAH 9:1-2)

Messiah entered this dark world to give it spiritual light. John the Baptist was sent by God as a forerunner, to testify of the Light; so that people might believe in Him. He was the fulfillment of God's call to Abraham and Israel, to be a blessing to all nations.

Fulfilment

Jesus began His ministry in Galilee, travelling through the region preaching repentance, teaching in the synagogues and healing the people of all their sicknesses. News spread about Him to all the surrounding regions and great crowds flocked to Him.

It was from the region of Galilee that Jesus began calling out fishermen to follow Him, promising to make them fishers of men.

Witness: Nathanael

When Nathanael heard about Jesus of Nazareth, knowing from Scripture that Messiah would be born in Bethlehem, he asked if anything good could come out of Nazareth. But after Jesus had spoken with him, Nathanael called Him Rabbi and declared that He was the Son of God and the King of Israel!

> *"The Spirit of the Lord GOD is upon Me,*
> *Because the LORD has anointed Me*
> *To preach good tidings to the poor;*
> *He has sent Me to heal the brokenhearted,*
> *To proclaim liberty to the captives,*
> *And the opening of the prison to those who are bound;*
> ***To proclaim the acceptable year of the LORD…"***
>
> (ISAIAH 61:1-2, EMPHASIS ADDED)

Fulfilment

On the Sabbath day, Jesus read this portion of Scripture

from Isaiah to the synagogue congregation in Nazareth. He told the people assembled there that the Scripture was now fulfilled. In applying these prophetic words to Himself, He was claiming to be the Messiah; as well as proclaiming the nature of His mission.

At first he was received well, but they also remembered that He was only Joseph and Mary's son. Jesus would not prove His claim by performing miraculous signs for them and He said that no prophet was welcome in his hometown.

There had been many widows in Israel during three years of drought, but God did not send Elijah the prophet to any of them, He had only sent him to help a widow in Zarephath, in the region of Sidon. There were many lepers in Israel in the time of Elisha the prophet, but only Naaman the Syrian was cleansed. After hearing this they were furious and dragged Jesus to a cliff edge, to throw Him over; but He calmly walked through the mob and went on His way.

Now Herod Antipas had divorced his wife, in order to marry his niece. John the Baptist had publicly condemned him for this sin and consequently Herod had ordered his arrest.

While in prison, John sent two of his disciples to Jesus, to ask whether He was the coming One, or should they continue waiting. John's surprising uncertainty was possibly caused by his expectations of a conquering Messiah, as most Jews were anticipating at that time. Perhaps he had even expected to be liberated from prison.

But Jesus was releasing captives of sin and performing miraculous healings. The blind could see, the lame could walk, and the deaf could hear! He also excelled in preaching and teaching the Gospel of Good News to the poor.

Witnesses: John's disciples

Jesus told John's disciples to report back to John with the evidence of what they had seen and heard of His ministry.

After their departure, Jesus praised John the Baptist, saying that he was a messenger from God and a great prophet. It was written about him in the Scriptures, the one who would come and prepare the way for Messiah's coming (Malachi 3:1).

Messiah's Entry into Jerusalem as King

"Rejoice greatly, O daughter of Zion!
Shout, O daughter of Jerusalem!
Behold, your King is coming to you;
He is just and having salvation,
Lowly and riding on a donkey,
A colt, the foal of a donkey."

(Zechariah 9:9)

Fulfilment

Jesus, knowing it would be His final journey, went up to Jerusalem with His disciples for the Passover feast. On this occasion He presented Himself publicly as the Messiah and King of Israel.

Witnesses: Disciples and Multitudes

As He rode towards Jerusalem on the foal of a donkey, the large crowds accompanying Him from Jericho cried out, *"Hosanna to the **Son of David**! 'Blessed is He who comes in the name of the*

LORD!' Hosanna in the highest!" (Matthew 21:9, Psalm 118:2; emphasis added)

As He drew near the city, knowing the future events that would happen to Jerusalem and her people, Jesus wept with great compassion. He said that a time would come when their enemies would destroy the city and not one stone of the temple would remain intact. They would not see Him again until they said, *"Blessed* is *He who comes in the name of the LORD!"* (Matthew 23:39)

When Jesus' procession entered Jerusalem, with the accompanying multitude loudly rejoicing and praising God, the whole city was shaken and wanted to know what was happening.

Jesus went straight to the temple and drove out those who were buying and selling there. In righteous anger, He overturned the tables of the money changers and the seats of those selling doves. And He said to them, *"It is written, 'My house shall be called a house of prayer,' but you have made it a 'den of thieves.'"* (Isaiah 56:7, Matthew 21:13)

WITNESSES: THE LAME, THE BLIND AND CHILDREN

Then the blind and lame came to Jesus in the temple and He healed them. But the chief priests and scribes were angered by Jesus' actions; and indignant when they heard the children shouting, "Hosanna to the **Son of David!**"

Jesus said to them, *"Yes. Have you never read, 'Out of the mouth of babes and nursing infants You have perfected praise'?"* (Psalm 8:2 and Matthew 21:16)

The ordinary and disreputable people had listened to John's message of repentance and were baptized. But the religious leaders had refused to listen to John, or submit to being baptized by him. These Jewish religious leaders also rejected and opposed Jesus. Throughout His ministry they had looked for a way to outwit and trap Him.

Jesus had publicly accused them of pretending to be pious, but secretly seeking prestige and power. He had condemned them as being blind guides, who neglected justice, mercy and truth. After Jesus' triumphal entry into Jerusalem as Messiah, they secretly plotted together to kill Him after the Passover Feast.

Israel Rejects the Gospel

Who has believed our report?
And to whom has the arm of the LORD been revealed?

(ISAIAH 53:1)

Fulfilment

Jesus, knowing that He had a redemptive purpose to accomplish at His first coming, had openly declared His predicted sufferings and death. But He also said that He would be victorious over death and spoke of His future glory. However, Jesus was mis-understood by the Jews when he said, *"Destroy this temple, and in three days I will raise it up"* (John 2:19). They thought that He was speaking of the temple building, but Jesus was speaking of the temple of His body.

When pressed by the Jews for a sign, Jesus spoke of Jonah, who was a sign of death and resurrection. Just as the prophet had been three days and three nights in the whale's belly; so He would be three days and three nights in the earth.

Jesus had also taught about the signs that would precede

His second coming. But at that time, His disciples did not fully comprehend the things He told them. Knowing that the appointed time of His suffering was drawing near, Jesus was troubled. He said that when He was lifted up from the earth, He would draw all peoples to Himself, signifying the way in which He would die.

The crowd, knowing the Scriptures that spoke of Messiah reigning triumphantly forever, questioned His statements. Even after all the miraculous signs and miracles they had witnessed, they did not believe in Him. Yet there were those who secretly believed, even among the leaders. But because of their fear of being put out of the synagogue, they kept quiet.

After His triumphal entry into Jerusalem and the confrontation in the temple, Jesus went to stay with friends in nearby Bethany. While Jesus was eating, a woman came in with an alabaster jar of pure spikenard and breaking the jar she poured all the contents on Jesus' head. His disciples, especially Judas, criticized her for wasting perfume that was worth a year's wages.

But Jesus defended the woman's action; she had poured oil on His body to anoint Him for burial. What she had done would be remembered and admired.

CHAPTER NINE

PROPHECIES OF
MESSIAH'S BETRAYAL

BETRAYED BY A FRIEND

Even my own familiar friend in whom I trusted,
Who ate my bread,
Has lifted up His heel against me.

(PSALM 41: 9)

FULFILMENT

After the meal at Bethany, Judas Iscariot went secretly to the chief priests. He asked what they would offer him to betray Jesus and they gave him thirty pieces of silver.

During the Passover meal with His disciples Jesus was troubled. He said that one of them was going to betray Him. The disciples were stunned, and each of them began to ask

Him if they were the one who would do this. Jesus said that it was the disciple to whom He would give a piece of bread, after dipping it in the dish. Then Jesus dipped the bread and gave it to Judas.

After receiving the piece of bread, Satan entered Judas and he left the room quickly. And it was night.

A New Covenant

> "Behold, the days are coming, says the LORD, when I will make a new covenant with the house of Israel and with the house of Judah…"
>
> (JEREMIAH 31:31)

FULFILMENT

Jesus took the bread and broke it. Then He gave it to the disciples; saying that the bread was His body. He took the cup of wine, gave thanks and told them to drink from it. He said that it was **His blood of the new covenant, which is shed for the forgiveness of sins**.

FORSAKEN BY HIS DISCIPLES

> "Awake, O sword, against My Shepherd,
> Against the Man who is My Companion,"
> Says the LORD of hosts.
> "Strike the Shepherd,
> And the sheep will be scattered;"
>
> (ZECHARIAH 13:7)

FULFILMENT

Jesus told His disciples that they would all forsake Him that night, as it was prophesied. Peter protested, stating that he would never deny Him. But Jesus said that night, before the rooster crows, he would deny Him three times.

Then Jesus went out with the disciples, to a place called Gethsemane. Deeply troubled, Jesus prayed to His Father, asking if it were possible for this cup of suffering to pass from Him. Nevertheless, not His will, but His Father's will be done.

As Jesus continued in anguished prayer, His disciples fell asleep.

Then He warned them to be alert, His time of betrayal was near. While He was still speaking Judas arrived, leading an armed crowd. He went straight to Jesus and identified Him to the guards with a kiss. When they seized Jesus, one of His disciples struck the high priest's servant and slashed off his ear.

But Jesus told him to put his sword away and restored the man's ear. He had all heaven's power at His disposal; but it was His Father's will that the Scriptures concerning Him were fulfilled. At this point all His disciples deserted Him and ran away.

Jesus was arrested and led away to the high priest's house, where all the scribes and elders had assembled. Peter followed at a distance and joined the guards sitting around a fire in the courtyard.

MESSIAH OPPRESSED AND AFFLICTED

He was oppressed and He was afflicted,
Yet He opened not His mouth;

(ISAIAH 53:7)

FULFILMENT

Throughout His unlawful arrest and trial, alone and undefended, Jesus acted with dignity. He remained silent as false witnesses came forward and told lies about Him.

Finally the high priest commanded Jesus, under oath to the living God, to say whether He was the Messiah, the Son of God. Jesus answered in the affirmative. Speaking prophetically of His second coming, He stated that He would be seen sitting at the right hand of God and coming on the clouds of heaven (Daniel 7:13).

Jesus was speaking truthfully, but the high priest accused Him of blasphemy and all those assembled there called for the death sentence. Then they began to spit in Jesus' face and beat Him. Having blindfolded Jesus, they mockingly asked Him to prophesy who it was who had struck Him.

Meanwhile, as Peter waited in the courtyard, a servant girl came to him and said that he had been with Jesus of Nazareth. But Peter denied it and said he didn't know what she was talking about. As he went out to the gateway another girl saw him and also said that he was with Jesus of Nazareth. But Peter swore that he did not know Him.

Later on other bystanders insisted that Peter was one of the disciples, because it was obvious from his speech that he was a Galilean. Peter began to swear and curse, saying he that he did not know the Man. While Peter was still speaking, a rooster crowed. Then he remembered Jesus telling him that before the rooster crows, he would deny Him three times. Then Peter left the courtyard, weeping bitterly.

To Be Sold for Thirty Pieces of Silver

And the LORD said to me, "Throw it to the potter" – that princely price they set on me. So I took the thirty pieces of silver and threw them into the house of the LORD for the potter.

(ZECHARIAH 11:13)

Fulfilment

Judas, seeing that Jesus was condemned, was overcome with remorse and returned the thirty pieces of silver to the chief priests and elders. He said that he had sinned in betraying an innocent man, but they were indifferent to his remorse. So Judas threw the coins into the temple, then he went out and hanged himself.

Knowing that it was unlawful to accept blood money as an offering in the temple, the chief priests decided to buy a plot of ground to bury strangers in, known as the potter's field.

CHAPTER TEN

PROPHECIES OF
MESSIAH'S SUFFERING

LAMBLIKE

*He was led as **a lamb to the slaughter**,*
And as a sheep before its shearers is silent,
So He opened not His mouth.

(ISAIAH 53:7, EMPHASIS ADDED)

FULFILMENT

The Jewish leaders had no authority to execute Jesus and the next morning He was taken to Pilate, to be tried in the Roman Court.

Pilate asked Jesus if He was the King of the Jews and Jesus answered that it was so. But during the incessant accusations from the chief priests and leaders, He remained silent.

Pilate was very impressed with Jesus and did not want to condemn an innocent man. It was the custom during the Passover feast for the Roman governor to release a prisoner. So Pilate asked the crowd who they wanted him to release. Should Jesus Barabbas, a notorious murderer and rebel against the Roman government, be set free; or Jesus, who was called Messiah?

The Jewish leaders had already persuaded the gathered mob against Jesus and they cried out for the release of Barabbas. When Pilate asked what he should do with Jesus, they all answered that he should be crucified. Pilate asked them why, seeing that Jesus had done no evil. But they continued to cry out for Him to be crucified.

Reason and justice had no influence on the mob. So Pilate washed his hands before them, saying that he had no responsibility for Jesus' death, it was their decision. Seeing that a riot was imminent, he reluctantly handed Jesus over to be scourged, a life threatening punishment.

MESSIAH DISFIGURED BEYOND RECOGNITION

Behold, My Servant shall deal prudently;
He shall be exalted and extolled and be very high.
Just as many were astonished at you,
So His visage was marred more than any man,
And His form more than the sons of men;

(ISAIAH 52:13-14)

FULFILMENT

After Jesus was scourged, the Roman soldiers took Him to the Praetorium and the whole garrison gathered around him. They dressed Jesus in a scarlet robe and pressed down a crown of thorns on His head. Then they placed a reed in His hand, as a mock scepter and they knelt before Him saying, *"Hail, King of the Jews!"* (Matthew 27:29). They spat on Jesus, took the reed from His hand and beat Him on the head with it.

The brutal punishment and abuse disfigured His appearance, until Jesus was no longer recognizable. After the soldiers had satisfied their sadistic pleasure, they took off the robe and returned His clothes to Him. Then He was led out to be crucified, the cruelest form of execution, reserved for the worst of criminals.

MESSIAH WAS TO BE PIERCED

For dogs have surrounded Me;
The congregation of the wicked has enclosed Me.
They pierced My hands and My feet;

(PSALM 22:16)

This psalm describes, 1000 years before Jesus was born, the crucifixion of Messiah, in complete and accurate detail.

FULFILMENT

Exhausted and weakened, Jesus was unable to carry His cross. One of the guards ordered a bystander, Simon from Cyrene, to carry Jesus' cross to Golgotha.

They offered Him a mixture of wine and myrrh to dull His pain, but after tasting it Jesus refused to drink. Then they nailed His hands and feet to the cross.

They Gambled For Messiah's Garments

They divide My garments among them,
And for My clothing they cast lots.

(Psalm 22:18)

Fulfilment

The executioners had the privilege of taking the victim's clothes. After crucifying Jesus, the soldiers threw dice for His garments. Above His head they had put a written sign of the criminal charge against Him.

THIS IS JESUS
THE KING OF THE JEWS

Messiah Crucified With Thieves

And He was numbered with the transgressors,
And He bore the sin of many,
And made intercession for the transgressors.

(Isaiah 53:12)

Fulfilment

Jesus was crucified with two robbers, one either side of Him, and all those passing by contemptuously blasphemed Him. Jesus experienced cruel rejection yet He responded with prayers for those who sinned against Him; asking His Father to forgive them, because they were acting in ignorance.

Messiah is Despised and Rejected

He is despised and rejected by men,
A Man of sorrows and acquainted with grief.
And we hid, as it were, our faces from Him;

(Isaiah 53:3a)

All those who see Me ridicule Me;
They shoot out the lip, they shake the head, saying,
"He trusted in the Lord, let Him rescue Him;
Let Him deliver Him, since He delights in Him!"

(Psalm 22:7-8)

Fulfilment

Those who passed by challenged Jesus to save Himself, if He really was the Son of God! The religious leaders observed His suffering with indifference and joined in with the mockery. They also defied Him to prove He was the Messiah, by coming down from the cross.

Messiah is a Sin Offering

But He was wounded for our transgressions,
He was bruised for our iniquities;
The chastisement for our peace was upon Him,
And by His stripes we are healed.
All we like sheep have gone astray;
We have turned, every one, to his own way;
And the Lord has laid on Him the iniquity of us all.

(Isaiah 53:5-6)

Fulfilment

Jesus' enemies continued to sneer, even the two robbers next to Him joined in the ridicule. What they did not understand, was that Jesus could not save Himself and save us at the same time! Therefore He chose to endure His suffering and remained on the cross.

Jesus had said when arrested in the garden, that if He had asked His Father, He would have provided twelve legions of angels. But it was necessary for Him to suffer and rise from the dead on the third day. To fulfill what was written about Him in the Law of Moses, the Prophets and the Psalms.

Messiah Feels Forsaken by God

My God, My God, why have You forsaken Me?

(Psalm 22:1)

Fulfilment

From the sixth hour (noon), there was a supernatural darkness over all the land for three hours, and Jesus was hidden from the gaping crowd. *About the ninth hour Jesus cried out with a loud voice, saying, "Eli, Eli, lama sabachthani?" that is, "My God, My God, why have You forsaken Me?"* (Matthew 27:46)

These words, spoken by Jesus in Aramaic, were written by David 1000 years previously.

Hearing Jesus' cry of abandonment, some of the bystanders thought He was calling for Elijah. God was not turning from His Son, but from the sins His Son was bearing for the whole world at that time. Jesus had always been with the Father and this must surely have caused Him to experience a most cruel sense of rejection and complete isolation.

MESSIAH THIRSTS

My strength is dried up like a potsherd,
And My tongue clings to My jaws;
You have brought Me to the dust of death.

(PSALM 22:15)

Reproach has broken my heart,
And I am full of heaviness;
I looked for someone to take pity, but there was none;
And for comforters, but I found none.
They also gave me gall for my food,
And for my thirst they gave me vinegar to drink.

(PSALM 69:20-21)

FULFILMENT

From the time of His arrest to being crucified, Jesus had endured six separate trials and extremely brutal punishment. On the cross He suffered agonizing pain, exhaustion and terrible thirst; as well as the emotional pain of scorn, rejection and isolation.

One of those standing by the cross ran and soaked a sponge with sour wine; then lifted it up on a stick for Him to drink. But others with him told him to not to bother. They wanted to see if Elijah would come and help Him.

CHAPTER ELEVEN

PROPHECIES OF MESSIAH'S DEATH AND BURIAL

MESSIAH GIVES UP HIS LIFE

Into Your hand I commit my spirit;

(PSALM 31:5)

FULFILMENT

In spite of His physical weakness and thirst, Jesus cried out with a loud voice, *"Father, 'into Your hands I commit My spirit.'"* (Luke 23:46)

Having accomplished His Father's will and finished His mission, Jesus yielded up His spirit to His Father. At that moment the veil of the temple, separating the holy place from the Most Holy Place, was torn in two from top to bottom;

God had made a direct and personal way of access to Himself through His Son's atoning death.

WITNESSES: THE CENTURION AND HIS SOLDIERS

There was an earthquake, rocks were split and many dead saints came back to life. When the centurion and the soldiers who were guarding Jesus saw these frightening supernatural signs, they were convinced that He truly was the Son of God.

WITNESSES: MANY WOMEN

There were many women who had followed Jesus from Galilee, and they were watching at a distance. Among them were Mary Magdalene, Mary the mother of James and Joses, and the mother of Zebedee's sons.

NOT ONE OF HIS BONES BROKEN

> *In one house it* (*the Passover lamb) *shall be eaten; you shall not carry any of the flesh outside the house, nor shall you break one of its bones.*
>
> (EXODUS 12:46, *AUTHOR'S NOTE)

It was the Preparation Day and the bodies could not remain on the crosses during Sabbath. So the Jews asked Pilate that their legs be broken to hasten death and their bodies taken away. So the soldiers broke the legs of the two crucified either side of Jesus; but seeing that Jesus was already dead, they did not break His legs.

Messiah's Side Is Pierced

"And I will pour on the house of David and on the inhabitants of Jerusalem the Spirit of grace and supplication; then they will look on Me whom they pierced."

(ZECHARIAH 12:10)

Fulfilment

One of the soldiers pierced Jesus' side with a spear; and blood and water poured out. In a future time the Jews would recognize the One who was pierced as the Messiah.

Buried With the Rich

And they made His grave with the wicked—
But with the rich at His death,
Because He had done no violence,
Nor was any deceit in His mouth.

(ISAIAH 53:9)

Fulfilment

It was the Roman custom to throw crucified bodies to the dogs. But Joseph of Arimathea, a rich man and a secret disciple of Jesus, asked Pilate for the body of Jesus. Pilate gave him permission and Joseph took the body away.

WITNESSES: JOSEPH OF ARIMATHEA AND NICODEMUS

Then Nicodemus, who was also a secret believer, came openly with myrrh and aloes. They covered Jesus' body with spices and bound it with clean linen cloths. Then they placed His body into Joseph's tomb, which he had recently cut into the rock. Afterwards they rolled a large stone across the entrance of the tomb.

The day after Preparation Day, the Jewish leaders went to Pilate and said that Jesus had claimed He would arise from the dead after three days. Therefore they asked for the tomb to be guarded until the third day. Otherwise His disciples might steal the body and deceive the people, claiming that Jesus had risen from the dead.

Pilate agreed to their request and told them to go and secure the tomb. So they sealed the stone across the entrance and put soldiers there to guard it.

CHAPTER TWELVE

PROPHECIES OF MESSIAH'S RESURRECTION

POWER OVER DEATH

For You will not leave my soul in Sheol,
Nor will You allow Your Holy One to see corruption.

(PSALM 16:10)

FULFILMENT

Early in the morning, on the first day of the week, Mary Magdalene and another woman named Mary came to the tomb. Suddenly, there was an earthquake and an angel of God descended from heaven.

He rolled away the stone from the entrance of the tomb and sat on it. Shafts of light shone from him and his garments were white as snow. The soldiers guarding the tomb were so frightened they could not move!

The angel told the women not to be afraid. Jesus was not there; He had risen, just as He had promised. The angel invited them to look into the empty tomb where Jesus had been laid. Then he told them to quickly go and tell the disciples that Jesus had risen and was going on ahead of them to Galilee.

WITNESSES: DISCIPLES

Full of wonder, the women left the tomb and ran to tell the disciples. Suddenly, Jesus met them and they fell to their knees, embracing His feet and worshiping Him. Jesus told them not to be afraid, but to tell His brothers to go to Galilee, and He would see them there.

Meanwhile, some of the guards returned to the city and told the high priests everything that had happened. The religious leaders urgently consulted together and came up with a plan. They gave the soldiers a large sum of money as a bribe, to say that Jesus' disciples had come at night and stolen His body while they were sleeping.

Later that day, the disciples were together in a locked room, because they were afraid of the Jews. Suddenly, Jesus stood among them, and said, *"Peace be with you."* Then He showed them His hands and His side (John 20:19).

Jesus said again, *"Peace to you! As the Father has sent Me, I also send you."* Then He breathed on them and told them to receive the Holy Spirit (John 20: 21).

Now Thomas was absent at the time and the other disciples told him they had seen the LORD. He said that, unless he saw and touched the wounds in Jesus' hands and side, he would not believe.

After eight days, Jesus came again to His disciples. He told Thomas to touch His wounds and to stop being unbelieving, but believing. *"And Thomas answered and said to Him, "My Lord and my God!" Jesus said to him, "Thomas, because you have seen Me, you have believed. Blessed are those who have not seen and yet have believed."* (John 20:28-29)

Witnesses: Over 500

In the early morning, after His resurrection, Jesus was seen by Mary Magdalene and other women. In the afternoon He appeared to two disciples on the way to Emmaus and also to Peter. In the evening He appeared to ten of His disciples, and a week later to His eleven disciples, including Thomas.

Sometime later Jesus appeared to seven of His disciples at Galilee and, at an unspecified time, He met with James. His final appearance to all His disciples was at His Ascension (Acts 1:3 and Acts 1: 11).

The apostle Paul records that Jesus was seen by Peter, and then by His other disciples. After that He was seen by more than five hundred brethren at once. At an unspecified time, he was seen by James; and then by all of the apostles. Last of all He was seen by Paul himself on the Damascus Road

(1 Corinthians 15:5-8 and Acts 9:3-6).

Victorious over Death

He will swallow up death forever,
And the Lord GOD will wipe away tears from all faces;
The rebuke of His people
He will take away from all the earth;
For the LORD has spoken.

(ISAIAH 25:8)

It was not such an incredible thing for God to raise the dead. Elisha the prophet miraculously brought a child back to life. And there was another miracle of resurrection when the body of a dead man was thrown on Elisha's grave; immediately the corpse touched the prophet's bones, the man was restored to life (2 Kings 4:34-35 and 2 Kings 13:20- 21).

During Jesus' ministry He raised Lazarus from the dead, and many Jews believed in Him because of this miracle. Jesus stated, *"I am the resurrection and the life. He who believes in Me, though he may die, he shall live. And whoever lives and believes in Me shall never die. Do you believe this?"* (John 11:25-26)

Through the atoning death of Jesus, all who believed in Him would be raised from death to eternal life.

Although there are many references to faith in resurrection recorded in the Bible, the Sadducees denied that there could be a resurrection and based their teaching solely on the five books of Moses.

One day, when Jesus was teaching in the temple, the Sadducees asked Him a question concerning the resurrection and marriage. Jesus had replied that for those who were included in the resurrection there was no marriage, they would be like angels of God.

He also pointed out that Moses had shown clearly that the dead are raised to life, in recording God's words to him from the burning bush: *Moreover He said, "I am the God of your father – the God of Abraham, the God of Isaac, and the God of Jacob."* (Exodus 3:6 and Matthew 22:23-33)

God was not the God of the dead, but of the living.

Fulfilment

During the forty days, from His victory over the grave to the day He was taken up to heaven, His disciples walked, talked and ate with their Risen Lord. Having fulfilled many of the Biblical prophecies; Jesus opened up their minds to understand all that the prophets had written about Him.

Jesus' glorified body had visible marks of the nails in His hands and feet, and the wound in His side. But in the power of His glorified body, Jesus was no longer subject to the limitations of human life.

Messiah's Ascension

Before Jesus' Ascension, He told His disciples that they would be His witnesses in Jerusalem, then in Judea and Samaria, and to the end of the earth. He instructed them to wait in Jerusalem until they had received the baptism of the Holy Spirit.

Witnesses: Eleven Disciples and others with them

His disciples were eager to know when He would restore the kingdom to Israel; but Jesus said that it was not for them to know the times set by His Father. After saying these things, while His disciples were watching, Jesus was taken up to heaven in a cloud.

Enoch did not experience death as his living earthly body was caught up to God. Also, while still living, Elijah the prophet was taken up to Heaven by angels. But Messiah rose from the dead and in a glorified body ascended to Heaven, as the Son of God. Enoch and Elijah ascended as servants of God.

MESSIAH IS OUR SAVIOUR

And it shall come to pass
That *whoever calls on the name of the LORD*
Shall be saved.

(JOEL 2:32)

Jesus' life was lived entirely dedicated to His Father's will. He was the perfect sacrificial Lamb of God, whose death and shed blood secured a perfect salvation for all those who would believe in Him.

"For the life of the flesh is in the blood, and I have given it to you upon the altar to make atonement for your souls; for it is blood that makes atonement for the soul."

(LEVITICUS 17:11)

For God so loved the world that He gave His only begotten Son, that whoever believes in Him should not perish but have everlasting life.

(JOHN 3:16)

CHAPTER THIRTEEN

PROPHECIES OF MESSIAH'S SECOND COMING

MESSIAH'S RETURN PROMISED

"Men of Galilee, why do you stand gazing up into heaven?
This same Jesus, who was taken up from you into heaven, will
so come in like manner as you saw Him go into heaven."

(ACTS 1:11)

At the end of His earthly ministry, Jesus met with His disciples on the Mount of Olives and instructed them to wait in Jerusalem, for the outpouring and baptism of the Holy Spirit. On hearing this, the disciples were concerned about when the kingdom would be restored to Israel. But Jesus told them that only the Father knew the dates and times, their focus must be on telling others about Him. They would receive power to witness when the Holy Spirit came upon them.

After Jesus had spoken these things and blessed them, He

was taken up to heaven in a cloud. And while His disciples were watching His ascent, two angels appeared to them and promised that Jesus would return in the same way that they had seen Him go. Daniel the prophet had a vision of Messiah's return to earth on the clouds of heaven (Daniel 7:13).

Messiah's second coming will be at a time when antichrist has already appeared on the political scene. As this charismatic and manipulative leader rises to dominant world power, he will make a treaty with Israel, gaining favour with the Jewish people.

But antichrist's deception and treachery will be revealed when he demands to be worshipped as God. The Jews will refuse to obey this blasphemous command and antichrist will turn on them in furious revenge; stirring up war against Israel and influencing worldwide persecution against Jews (Daniel 9:27 and 11:36).

ALL NATIONS GATHER AGAINST ISRAEL

> *"And it shall happen in that day that I will make Jerusalem a very heavy stone for all peoples; all who would heave it away will surely be cut in pieces, though all nations of the earth are gathered against it."*

> (ZECHARIAH 12:3)

This universal attack will be disastrous for Israel; two out of every three Jews will be killed, but a third will be saved by divine mercy and intervention.

Jeremiah spoke of these future events. *"Alas! For that day is great, so that none is like it; and it is the time of Jacob's trouble, but he shall be saved out of it."* (Jeremiah 30:7)

Daniel also prophesied concerning this period, *"And there shall be a time of trouble, such as never was since there was a nation, even to that time. And at that time your people shall be delivered, everyone who is found written in the book."* (Daniel 12:1)

GOD'S DAY OF VENGEANCE

"To proclaim the acceptable year of the LORD,
And the day of vengeance for our God;"

(ISAIAH 61:2)

At the beginning of the Jesus's public ministry, full of the Holy Spirit, He returned to Galilee and taught in the synagogues. When He went into the synagogue in Nazareth on the Sabbath day and stood up to read, He was handed the book of the prophet Isaiah.

Reading from the beginning of chapter 61, Jesus declared the following words: *"The Spirit of the Lord GOD is upon Me, because the LORD has anointed Me to preach good tidings to the poor; He has sent Me to heal the brokenhearted, to proclaim liberty to the captives, and the opening of the prison to those who are bound; to proclaim the acceptable year of the LORD…"*

Then He closed the book in the middle of the sentence and sat down. He did not continue reading because He was the fulfillment of those prophetic words. He was the long awaited Messiah, the time of God's mercy and favour had come to Israel.

The next phrase, referring to the day of God's vengeance, would be fulfilled at the time of Messiah's second coming.

Messiah Will Return with the Saints

Then the Lord will go forth
And fight against those nations,
As He fights in the day of battle.
And in that day His feet will stand on the Mount of Olives,
Which faces Jerusalem on the east.
And the Mount of Olives shall be split in two,
From east to west,
Making *a very large valley;*
Half of the mountain will move toward the north
And half of it toward the south.
Then you shall flee through *My mountain valley,*
for the mountain valley shall reach to Azal.
Yes, you shall flee
As you fled from the earthquake
In the days of Uzziah king of Judah.

(Zechariah 14: 3-5)

When God judged the nation of Egypt with a series of plagues, this forced Pharaoh to release His people. After Moses had led the Hebrews out of Egypt, Pharaoh changed his mind, and accompanied by the Egyptian army, pursued his former slaves.

By this time the Hebrew people were camping at the Red Sea. Trapped between the advancing army and the sea, there was nowhere to flee. But God Himself intervened and miraculously parted the waters, making a way of escape for His people.

He also destroyed the Egyptians that pursued them into the sea, by bringing the waters back together and drowning them (Exodus 15:3-5).

In like manner, at a future time, when all human hope for

Israel's survival has gone, God Himself will intervene. He will bring judgment on the attacking nations with a supernatural plague on their bodies and minds. And in their confusion they will fight against each other. He will also make a way of escape for the survivors of His people (Zechariah 14: 12-13).

Spirit of Grace and Supplication

> *"And I will pour on the house of David and on the inhabitants of Jerusalem the Spirit of grace and supplication; then they will look on Me whom they pierced. Yes, they will mourn for Him as one mourns for his only son, and grieve for Him as one grieves for a firstborn."*
>
> (Zechariah 12:10)

At the same time, He will show mercy on the remnant of Israel and The Holy Spirit will bring revelation to their hearts. They will know that the One they rejected and crucified is their Messiah. The result of this understanding will be deep repentance, they will mourn bitterly, as for a first-born son.

Spiritual Cleansing and Renewal

> *"In that day a fountain shall be opened for the house of David and for the inhabitants of Jerusalem, for sin and for uncleanness."*
>
> (Zechariah 13:1)

There will also be a spiritual cleansing for the land and people. All forms of idolatry will be banished and any false prophet continuing to practice these things will be put to death

(Deuteronomy 18:20). Purged and refined, Jerusalem will emerge as the holy city of God.

> *Thus the LORD my God will come,*
> And *all the saints with You.*

(ZECHARIAH 14: 5)

MESSIAH DESCENDS ONTO THE MOUNT OF OLIVES

At some point during these events, Messiah will descend onto the Mount of Olives with innumerable angels and resurrected believers. His coming will cause momentous geological changes. There will be an earthquake and the Mount of Olives will split in two, making a valley by which the besieged survivors can escape.

Jerusalem will be raised up and leveled off, becoming the highest mountain in the area. An event also foretold by the prophets Isaiah and Micah (Isaiah 2:2 and Micah 4:1).

COSMIC UPHEAVAL

> *It shall come to pass in that day*
> That *there will be no light;*
> *The lights will diminish.*

(ZECHARIAH 14:6)

Before the days of the glorious reign of Messiah, there will be cosmic upheavals and dark days of judgment; a time like no other in earth's history (Joel 2:10-11, Malachi 3:2-3).

GOD THE GLORY OF HIS PEOPLE

"The sun shall no longer be your light by day,
Nor for brightness shall the moon give light to you;
But the LORD will be to you an everlasting light,
And your God your glory."

(ISAIAH 60:19)

This time of darkness will be followed by the light of Messiah's kingdom reign on earth. In that day, as a result of the geological changes, fountains will burst forth. Jerusalem will become a source of living water that will flow into two rivers. One will flow towards the Dead Sea and the other to the Mediterranean Sea; irrigating the land both summer and winter.

Ezekiel prophesied that this river will bring life and healing wherever it flows (Ezekiel 47: 9).

CHAPTER FOURTEEN

PROPHECIES OF MESSIAH'S EVERLASTING KINGDOM

Yet I have set My King
On My holy hill of Zion.

PSALM 2:6

Then to Him was given dominion and glory and a kingdom,
That all peoples, nations, and languages should serve Him.
His dominion is *an everlasting dominion,*
Which shall not pass away,
And His kingdom the one
Which shall not be destroyed.

(DANIEL 7:14)

And the LORD *shall be King over all the earth.*
In that day it shall be –
"The LORD *is one,"*
And His name one.

(ZECHARIAH 14:9)

King David prophesied that Messiah would reign as King, on the throne of David in Jerusalem and all those who rebelled against Him would perish. (Psalm 2:7-12)

Daniel spoke of Messiah having an everlasting kingdom and exercising absolute rule over all the nations. Zechariah prophesied that a day would come when Messiah would be King over all the earth.

MESSIAH THE RIGHTEOUS KING

"Behold, the days are coming," says the LORD,
"That I will raise to David a Branch of righteousness;
A King shall reign and prosper,
And execute judgment and righteousness in the earth."

(JEREMIAH 23:5)

And it shall come to pass that everyone who is left of all the nations which came against Jerusalem shall go up from year to year to worship the King, the LORD of hosts, and to keep the Feast of Tabernacles.

(ZECHARIAH 14:16)

Messiah will judge the nations with perfect righteousness. Repentant and believing people among those nations that attacked Jerusalem will worship the King and celebrate the Feast of Tabernacles. Those nations who are unwilling to worship the King and attend the yearly thanksgiving feast will experience God's judgment (Micah 4:2).

During Messiah's reign the people of Judah and Jerusalem will fulfill their destiny, as a holy priesthood belonging to God.

Remember the former things of old,
For I am *God, and there is no other;*
I am *God, and there is none like Me,*
Declaring the end from the beginning,
And from ancient times things that are not yet done,
Saying, 'My counsel shall stand,
And I will do all My pleasure.'

(Isaiah 46:9-10)

In the beginning was the Word
And the Word was God.
When He created you and me
In His image,
He created us in love.
We were created for His pleasure,
To love Him and each other.
His peace surround you,
His love uphold you,
Shalom, Shalom.

ABOUT THE AUTHOR

After studying at Art College and gaining a degree in Art and Design Pauline Shone began her working life as a teacher. But a commission from Spode China propelled her into a career as a freelance designer and sculptor for the ceramic industry. She worked for several other pottery factories over the following twenty years, but she is mainly known by her work for Spode China.

Not long after becoming a Christian this successful career came to a sudden and unexpected end. After a period in the wilderness, in obedience to God's calling on her life, she attended Torchbearers Bible College and became involved with missions.

Some years later, God used her creativity to write and illustrate Children's Bible Stories. There are currently 18 books in the series and over 400,000 have been distributed, mainly in India and China. Her desire and focus is to creatively communicate the truth of God's Word.

Pauline has a son and daughter, as well as four grandchildren.